This copy made possible by a generous
donation to the
Jackson County Library Foundation
from **Sherm and Wanda Olsrud.**

# Pyramids

Other books in the Wonders of the World series include:

The Eastern Island Statues
Gems
Geysers
The Grand Canyon
The Great Barrier Reef
Icebergs
King Tut's Tomb
Mummies
Niagara Falls
Quicksand
Sand Dunes
Sunken Treasures

# Pyramids

Teresa Hyman

**KIDHAVEN PRESS**

*An imprint of Thomson Gale, a part of The Thomson Corporation*

THOMSON

────★────
™

GALE

*For more information, contact*
KidHaven Press
27500 Drake Rd.
Farmington Hills, MI 48331-3535
Or you can visit our Internet site at http://www.gale.com

**LIBRARY OF CONGRESS CATALOGING-IN-PUBLICATION DATA**

Hyman, Teresa L.
  Pyramids / by Teresa Hyman.
    p. cm. — (Wonders of the world)
  Includes bibliographical references and index.
  ISBN 0-7377-2055-7 (alk. paper)
  1. Pyramids—Egypt—Juvenile literature. 2. Pyramids—Juvenile literature. I. Title.
II. Wonders of the world (Kidhaven Press)
  DT63.H935 2004
  932—dc22

                                                                    2004012063

Printed in the United States of America

# CONTENTS

# Pyramids of Treasure

**P**yramids have fascinated people for thousands of years. Today, pyramids are found everywhere—from the Louvre Museum in Paris, to the back of a U.S. one dollar bill. Thousands of years ago pyramids were a part of daily life for many people around the world. These ancient pyramids can be found in Africa, the Middle East, Asia, Central America, and South America. Scientists have studied these structures for centuries, trying to discover why and how they were built. The most famous of all ancient pyramids are the pyramids located in the deserts of Egypt.

Ancient Egyptians built over ninety pyramids from about 2630 B.C. until around 1530 B.C. These pyramids were built as burial places for Egyptian kings, queens, and other royal or rich Egyptians. The first Egyptian pyramid was built in Saqqara, a large citylike cemetery located in the Egyptian desert. It was built by an **archi-**

**tect** named Imhotep as a tomb for the Egyptian king Djoser, who ruled Egypt in the 2600s B.C.

## Imhotep's Step Pyramid

Before Imhotep's pyramid, Egyptian tombs were low-lying, rectangular-shaped brick monuments called **mastabas**. Burial chambers were located under the mastaba and were surrounded by many other chambers and storerooms. King Djoser wanted Imhotep to build him a much grander tomb than a mastaba. He wanted his tomb to be seen by all those who traveled to the capital city. He also wanted it to keep his treasures safe from thieves and grave robbers. So, instead of building the low, rectangular mastaba, Imhotep built the king a **step pyramid**.

Imhotep started with a mastaba base—a rectangle—and enlarged it on two sides to form a square. Then, he

The ancient pyramids found in the deserts of Egypt are the most famous of the world's pyramids.

built up, adding a smaller square on top of the base, then a smaller square on top of that one, and so on, creating six levels or steps. When it was finished, the pyramid was almost 200 feet (60.96 meters) high. It towered over the mastabas in Saqqara and could be seen by all travelers entering the city of Memphis. Djoser's dream of an impressive burial monument had come true.

Imhotep's design was the first of its kind in Egypt. It was unique not only because it was shaped like a pyramid instead of a rectangle, but also because it used stones instead of bricks. Imhotep had his workers haul limestone from a nearby quarry for the internal stones of the pyramid. For the pyramid's white surface, Imhotep had limestone from the faraway Tura cliff shipped across the Nile River to the pyramid building site.

Imhotep, an Egyptian architect, designed and built this step pyramid for King Djoser in the 2600s B.C.

The Great Pyramid of Khufu is the largest pyramid in Egypt, standing nearly 485 feet.

Imhotep's new stone design also hid the king's tomb. Instead of burying the tomb under the base of the pyramid, like in a mastaba, Imhotep hid the tomb inside the pyramid. He even built fourteen different entrances to fool grave robbers. Only one of the entrances led to the burial chamber and the storerooms filled with the king's treasures.

Egyptian rulers who followed Djoser also built large, impressive monuments as their burial chambers. They followed Imhotep's lead and used stone instead of brick for their pyramid-shaped tombs. But these rulers, or **pharaohs**, built larger, more elaborate tombs with flat surfaces instead of steps. In fact, Hemianu, architect of Pharaoh Khufu, built the largest pyramid in all of Egypt.

Called the Great Pyramid, it is made up of almost 2.5 million stones and stood almost 485 feet (147.82 meters) tall when it was completed. Hemianu made the stones for Khufu's pyramid fit together so perfectly that even today a piece of paper cannot fit between the massive stones!

## Treasures Within

The pyramid tombs of ancient Egypt were believed to help the dead cross over from the land of the living to the afterlife. Ancient Egyptians believed that a person's spirit left the body at death, only to return to it in the afterlife. In order for a person to be happy in the afterlife, the person needed everything that made life in the land of the living enjoyable. This included clothing, furniture, games, and even pets. Everything needed for the afterlife was stored in the pyramid. Even the walls of the pyramids were decorated with pictures of everyday life. It was believed that once the spirit of the dead person crossed over into the afterlife, the pictures would come alive.

When a wealthy Egyptian or an Egyptian ruler died, the person's pyramid tomb was prepared for the journey to the afterlife. Detailed **hieroglyphics** were painted on the burial chamber walls. These ancient writings and pictures celebrated the person's life and gave tribute to the many gods the Egyptians worshipped. They described what the person's life was like in the land of the living and the journey the dead person's spirit would take through the underworld. The Egyptians believed that Osiris, the god of the dead, would bring these scenes to life once the dead person crossed over into the afterlife.

These hieroglyphics helped early **Egyptologists** understand the daily life of ancient Egyptians.

## Preparing for the Afterlife

While the inside of the pyramid was being prepared, the dead person's body was prepared for the afterlife through **mummification**. For almost seventy days, priests performed sacred rituals and ceremonies that preserved the body. First, the body was washed, then cut open along the left side. The internal organs were removed and stored in clay pots called canopic jars. The heart, which

In this wall painting, the Egyptian god of the dead, Anubis, prepares the body of a pharaoh for the afterlife.

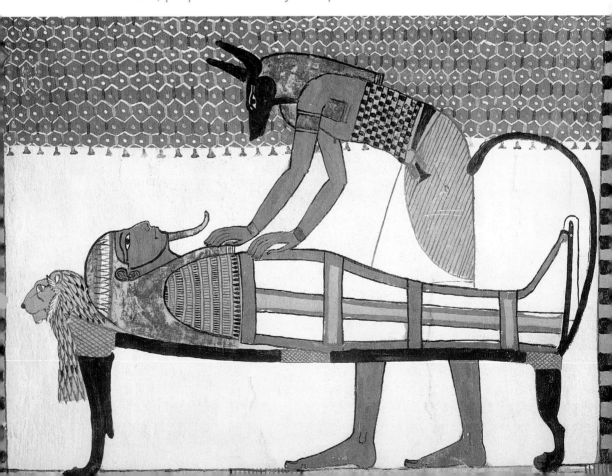

the Egyptians believed was the source of intelligence, was left in the body. The brain was pulled out a little at a time with a wire hook inserted into the corpse's nose. After removing the organs, the body was washed again and stuffed with scented spices and wine.

Priests would then use natron, a salt found along the Nile River, to dry the body and prevent it from decaying. The salt absorbed all the moisture in the body, leaving it dry and shriveled, but safe from rot and bacteria. After it was dried out, the body was rubbed with lotion made from oil, more natron, and wax to keep the skin from cracking. Then, the corpse was stuffed with sand, saw-

Mummification protected the body from decay. Even after thousands of years, the body of this mummy is very well preserved.

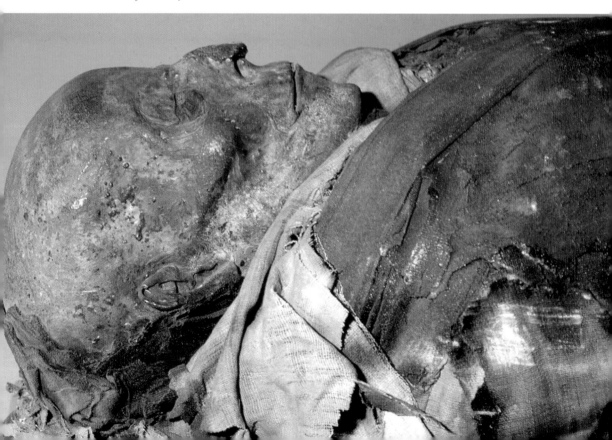

dust, and rags to make it appear thick, and the hole in the side was sewn closed. Finally, it was wrapped in linen cloth and coated with **resin** to keep it waterproof. At the end of the seventy days, the body was placed in a coffin, or **sarcophagus,** and sent to the tomb for burial.

Once the mummified body reached the tomb, all had been made ready. During the seventy days of preparing the body, the hieroglyphics would have been completed and the tomb filled with the earthly treasures needed for the afterlife. Clothing, fine jewels, makeup, perfumes, and books would have been arranged neatly within the storerooms of the pyramid. There would also be needles and thread for sewing, boats for traveling, tools for building, and pots for cooking. Some Egyptians even had their favorite pets or sacred animals, such as cats, dogs, birds, and crocodiles, mummified and buried with them. Finally, the body and its worldly treasures were sealed inside the pyramid to begin the journey to the afterlife. Priests, religious leaders, and members of the dead person's family would perform ceremonies in temples near the pyramid to help the dead person's spirit travel safely to the afterlife.

Ancient Egyptians built pyramids until around 1530 B.C., when expensive labor and materials and unstable governments made pyramid building almost impossible. Although the Egyptian pyramids are the most famous pyramids of ancient times, other ancient cultures also built monuments in the shape of pyramids. Although most had religious meanings, some pyramids combined religion with symbols of wealth and power.

# Pyramids of Power

**L**ocated in Sudan, just south of the pyramids of ancient Egypt, are the pyramids of another ancient African culture. These are the pyramids of Nubia. Built by black African rulers more than eight hundred years after the last pyramids in Egypt were built, the pyramids of Nubia represented the power of the Nubian gods as well as the power of the Nubian rulers.

## The People of Nubia

More than eleven thousand years ago, **nomads** hunted and fished along the upper portion of the Nile River. Eventually, these people abandoned their nomadic lifestyle. They settled in small communities along the southern regions of the river, from modern-day Egypt through Sudan. Taking advantage of the plentiful fish and shellfish of the Nile's waters and the fertile soil along its banks, these early Nubians established communities.

Ancient Nubians inhabited a land rich in semi-precious stones such as amethyst, jasper, and carnelian. Their land was also a rich source of iron. In fact, the Nubians were the first civilization to melt down iron to craft jewelry, tools, and weapons. It was here that precious minerals such as gold and copper were discovered, mined, and crafted into beautiful jewelry and fine adornments for clothing and hair. Gold was so important to the Nubian way of life that early historians and anthropologists took the name for these people and their culture—Nubia—from the Egyptian word for gold, *nub*.

The ancient Nubians settled small communities like this one along the southern regions of the Nile River.

Ancient Nubia was the source of all Egypt's riches. Nubians traded goods such as ebony, leopard skins, ostrich feathers, ivory, and gold for goods found in Egypt. These included honey, beer, wine, and linen. Nubian ironworkers forged weapons and tools for the Egyptians

These models of Nubian warriors armed with bows and arrows were found in an Egyptian tomb.

and traded them to their northern neighbors. Nubians also made up a large force of the Egyptian armies because they were highly skilled warriors and experts with the bow and crossbow. In these ways Egypt and Nubia needed each other to survive. Nubia provided Egypt with its gold, mineral riches, iron, and soldiers, while Egypt provided the smaller Nubian kingdoms with protection. But a peaceful existence was not to be.

Around 1500 B.C., Egyptian rulers became jealous of Nubia's power and riches. Egypt overpowered its smaller southern neighbor and ruled Nubia for over a thousand years. However, in 722 B.C., when Egypt was at the weakest in its history, Piye, a Nubian warrior, invaded and conquered Egypt. Nubian pharaohs then ruled Egypt for some sixty years—years anthropologists call the Twenty-fifth Dynasty of Egypt.

## Honoring the Pharaoh

After Piye's death, he was buried in his native Nubia. In the ancient Egyptian style, a pyramid was built in his honor. Although Egyptians had stopped building pyramids over eight hundred years before they were conquered by the Nubians, their Nubian cousins had reinvented this style of tribute.

Nubian pyramids were much smaller than the pyramids of ancient Egypt. For example, the largest Nubian pyramid, the pyramid of Taharqa, has a base of 170 square feet (15.79 square meters). The smallest of the Egyptian pyramids at Giza, the pyramid of Menkaure, has a base of 344 square feet (31.95 square meters).

Nubians also had a luxury their ancient Egyptian relatives did not have. They had a tool called a ***shadouf*** to help them build the pyramids. The *shadouf* was a crane used to lift the large stones the Nubians used to build their pyramids. Because of the way the *shadouf* was built, and the angle at which the stones were lifted and placed, Nubian pyramids were also much steeper than the earlier pyramids of ancient Egypt. Though some Nubian pyramids are step pyramids and others have smooth sides, all Nubian pyramids have three important parts. They have the pyramid, the underground burial chamber, and the temple located on the eastern wall of the pyramid.

Nubian pyramids like these in Sudan were much steeper than the pyramids of ancient Egypt.

The Nubians believed that their king was a child of the sun god Ra (center).

## Like the Sun

Ancient Nubians believed that their king was the son of Ra, the sun god, and, like the sun, the king's life followed a set pattern. When the king was young, his life was like the rising sun. When the king reached adulthood, he was at his full power and strength like the sun at noon. When the king grew old, he was like the setting sun. And when the king died, he was compared to the sun disappearing below the horizon. The sun traveled through the underworld in order to be reborn at the dawn of a new day. The dead king did just the same. Nubians believed that his

Pictured is a *shabti*, a statue buried with kings that came alive in the afterlife to serve the dead ruler.

soul would travel through the underworld toward the east, where it would be reborn into the afterlife.

Nubian pyramids reflected these beliefs. The pyramid represented the king's life cycle and ensured him a path to the afterlife. It was viewed as a ladder that the king's spirit would use to climb out of the underworld, up and into the afterlife.

## Serving the Dead

Beneath the steep, stone pyramid rested the mummified remains of the dead Nubian ruler. Mummified in the tradition of ancient Egypt, the mummy was placed on a flat slab of stone or in a highly decorated coffin in a large burial chamber directly beneath the top of the pyramid. The mummy was decorated with gold jewelry such as necklaces, rings, belts, and coverings for the hands, fingers, and toes. A gold or silver mask, carved and decorated to resemble the dead ruler, was also placed on the mummy's face.

Other chambers beneath the pyramid were filled with items the ruler would need in the afterlife. Clothing, jewelry, games, furniture, books, paintings, chests of gold and perfumes, fabrics, even food, were piled into the underground chambers. Kings and queens were often buried with small stone statues called *shabtis*. These *shabtis* would be brought to life by the god Osiris and made to serve the dead ruler in the afterlife. Toward 300 B.C., however, the *shabtis* were replaced by living servants who were mummified alive! Their bodies were placed in the burial chamber alongside the king or queen.

To ensure the ruler a safe passage through the underworld, sacrifices were made to Ra, Osiris, Isis, and other gods and goddesses of Nubian culture. Priests and others would travel to the pyramid temple to offer sacrifices and prayers. The doors to the temple would always be open and were decorated with paintings of the dead ruler. Within the temple, illustrations of the ruler's achievements in this life and travels through the underworld lined the walls. Illustrations of the gods and goddesses decorated the inner walls as well, and beautiful statues of the dead ruler adorned the temple. Visitors to the temple would bring gifts such as food, gold, or small animals for the gods. They would burn candles and incense and pray that the spirit of the ruler would find its way safely to the afterlife.

The pyramids of ancient Nubia were tributes to the power of the Nubian rulers and their gods. Viewed as ways to transport the spirit to the afterlife, the pyramids and temples were adorned with the riches that made the Nubians so powerful and were decorated with the images of their gods. Other ancient pyramids around the world were also tributes to powerful beliefs and ways of life.

# CHAPTER THREE

# Pyramid of Enlightenment

Thousands of miles from the pyramids of ancient Egypt and Nubia lies Angkor Wat. Angkor Wat is a massive, pyramid-shaped Hindu temple near the city of Siem Reap in Cambodia. The temple is considered a masterpiece of architecture. Covering nearly 1 square mile (2.6 square kilometers), it is the world's largest religious monument. It also houses the largest collection of Hindu carvings found anywhere.

The temple was built hundreds of years ago in the shape of the mythological home of the Hindu gods. The moat that surrounds it and each level, tower, column, and corridor represent a sacred place in that world. Those who entered Angkor Wat would have walked through its many rooms on a journey toward **enlightenment**. Enlightenment is a state of spiritual and emotional well-being. It is something that devout Hindus try to achieve during their lifetime.

## A Massive Undertaking

Like other Hindu temples, Angkor Wat is built in the shape of a mandala. A mandala looks like squares stacked one on top of the other, each smaller than the next. In

Angkor Wat, a Hindu temple complex in Cambodia, is the world's largest religious monument.

A team of French scientists sits on the steps of a temple in Angkor Wat during an expedition in 1868.

this way, the mandala is similar to a step pyramid. But this is where the similarity ends.

Angkor Wat is surrounded by a huge moat. It has three levels, each smaller than the next as they rise in height. Each level is made up of small buildings connected by terraces. Five huge lotus-shaped towers adorn the second and third levels of the pyramid and rise hundreds of feet in the air. The towers feature an elaborate design and are covered with gold leaf. The massive temple covers 4,265 feet (1,300 meters) from north to south and 4,921 feet (1,500 meters) from east to west. Its central tower measures 213 feet (65 meters) above the ground.

Angkor Wat was built around 1113 by Suryavarman, the king of the Khmer people. Construction took about thirty years to complete. A project of this size required thousands of slaves, builders, carvers, and artists. It also required huge quantities of building materials.

Sandstone was taken from quarries many miles away and brought to the site on riverboats and barges. Cambodian legends say that it took over seven hundred bamboo rafts and more than forty thousand elephants to move the stones from the different quarries to the site of the temple. Once there, the stones were cut into shape and decorated with detailed carvings. Over six thousand architects then worked to fit the stones into place. Experts believe it took as much stone to build Angkor Wat as it took to build the Great Pyramid in Egypt.

## A Jewel in the Jungle

Despite its huge size, Angkor Wat's location was unknown for hundreds of years. The Khmer people abandoned it in 1432 after they were invaded by a neighboring people. During that time, the overgrown vines and trees of the surrounding jungle swallowed the temple and hid it from view.

Angkor Wat was rediscovered by a French scientist in 1861, during a time when the French ruled Cambodia. Many French scientists traveled to the country to study the language and customs of its people and the plants and animals found there. Cambodians told the French stories of a city "built by the gods" somewhere in the dense Cambodian jungles. Most people thought the stories were simply

Angkor Wat is dedicated to Vishnu, a god Hindus worship as the preserver of the world.

legends, but one scientist believed them. Henri Mahout was determined to find the lost city, and in 1861 he did.

Mahout and his search team chopped through the thick Cambodian jungle and stumbled upon the outer wall of an ancient building. The team eventually discovered several buildings, but one stood out from the rest. That building, a pyramid, towered over the others and contained beautifully crafted stone carvings. That structure was the temple of Angkor Wat.

## A Tribute to Vishnu

Angkor Wat is dedicated to the Hindu god Vishnu. According to Hindu beliefs, Vishnu is the preserver of the world. He rests when all is right with the world, but rises

An enormous statue of Vishnu with flowers draped over his arms stands in a shrine at Angkor Wat.

to fight against evil when there is disorder. In paintings and sculptures he is usually portrayed with blue or black skin and four arms.

Many of Angkor Wat's features are symbols of Vishnu. Carved snakes and other animals associated with Vishnu, such as lions, turtles, and fish, adorn the temple walls. The five large towers are shaped like the buds of the lotus flower Vishnu carries in one of his four hands. Hundreds of carvings of Vishnu decorate the towers' surfaces, and many statues of the god once decorated the pyramid's halls.

Other Hindu gods are also depicted at Angkor Wat. A sacred lingam, or statue, representing the spirit of Shiva is found at the center of the pyramid temple. Shiva is the main god in Hindu belief. Shiva's lingam is at the center of Angkor Wat, just as Shiva is at the center of the Hindu universe.

## Bas-Relief Carvings

The thousands of carvings on the stones at Angkor Wat represent stories from ancient Hindu legends. Researchers believe that more than four hundred thousand craftsmen lent their talents to the creation of the elaborate illustrations. The carvings were created in a style called **bas-relief**. In this style, carved images are raised off the surface of the stone. These bas-relief carvings adorn every wall of the temple. They tell stories of love, of war, and of the creation of the Hindu universe.

The most famous and most detailed of the Angkor Wat carvings is called the Churning of the Ocean of

Pictured is a section from the most detailed and famous stone carving at Angkor Wat, the Churning of the Ocean of Milk.

Milk. This series of carvings extends down one hallway for more than 164 feet (50 meters).

In the carvings a giant snake coils around a mountain. The mountain is located in the middle of a great sea. In different scenes, gods and demons pull at opposite ends

Modern dancers in traditional dress perform for a group of tourists at Angkor Wat.

of the snake, as if in a great game of tug-of-war. The carvings show that as the snake is pulled this way and that, the mountain spins and giant waves form in the sea. The churning of the sea causes the sun and the moon to form. Beautiful fairylike creatures called *apsaras* are created along with Lakshmi, the goddess of beauty. The furious tugging of the gods and demons threatens to destroy the moon, the sun, and the entire universe. In the final scenes, Vishnu appears. He commands the gods and demons to work together. When they do, the universe is saved.

## Angkor Wat Today

Angkor Wat is still an important part of Cambodian culture. Today, three of Angkor Wat's five towers can be seen on Cambodia's national flag. Thousands of Hindu pilgrims and tourists visit Angkor Wat each year. They marvel at its size. They rub the stone carvings of the *apsaras* for luck. They pay tribute to Vishnu by leaving gifts of flowers.

Unlike Angkor Wat, some ancient pyramids did not focus on enlightenment. Instead, they focused on death as a way of satisfying the needs of the gods.

# CHAPTER
# FOUR

# Pyramid of Sacrifice

**O**n the Yucatán Peninsula of Mexico stands a limestone step pyramid built to honor the serpent god Kukulkan. The pyramid of Kukulkan is located in the ancient Mayan city of Chichén Itzá. Like other pyramids found in Mexico, Guatemala, Belize, and Honduras, this one once served as an important center of religious and social activity. It was a place for Mayan priests to study the stars and for farmers to plan their plantings and harvests. Above all, it was a place of worship. Here, Mayans honored their gods through human sacrifice.

## Pyramid of the Serpent God

The pyramid of Kukulkan was built sometime between the eleventh and thirteenth centuries on the ruins of older Mayan temples. It stands 79 feet (24 meters) high and is made from limestone, a hard rock found all around and under Chichén Itzá.

No one knows exactly how this pyramid was built. The Mayans did not have metal tools, pack animals, or even the wheel to help them build the pyramid of Kukulkan. One theory suggests that the Mayans applied a plant extract to the stones before carving to make them easier to shape. Another theory is that the Mayans traded with other cultures and acquired rocks harder than limestone, such as granite, to cut and chisel the limestone.

The Mayans built the limestone step pyramid in Chichén Itzá to honor their serpent god Kukulkan.

The stone sculptures of feathered serpents' heads, representing Kukulkan, lie on each side of the main stairway at its base.

These and other theories have not been proven, however.

As in other step pyramids, the first level of the pyramid of Kukulkan is the largest. Each level above gets smaller and smaller. A small temple tops off the structure. The main stairway is on the northern side of the pyramid. On either side of the main stairway, at the base, are stone sculptures of feathered serpents' heads. The heads represent Kukulkan.

Near the sculpted heads is the entrance to the pyramid's sanctuary. The entrance is divided into three doors by two columns shaped like snakes. Inside, two large pillars decorated with intricate carvings of Mayan warriors support the vaulted ceiling. Here, scientists discovered a stone statue of Chaac-Mool, the messenger of the gods. Chaac-Mool is reclining, its face turned to one side. Sharp pieces of shells adorn its eyes, fingernails, and teeth. A bowl rests on its knees. It is thought that the bowl was used to collect the blood or still-beating hearts of humans sacrificed to the gods.

## Feeding the Gods

According to the beliefs of the ancient Mayans, humans had to feed the gods. The nourishment the gods required was human blood. Most human blood offered to the Mayan gods was given voluntarily, and without killing the person who made the offering. A priest, priestess, or member of the ruling class would pierce a part of his or her body. The blood that flowed from the piercing was collected in bowls filled with sacred pieces of paper. When the paper and blood was burned, the Mayans believed, the blood would rise up and feed the gods. At times, the collected blood was also smeared on carvings or statues of the gods. This increased the chances of the gods receiving their "food."

Not all blood offerings were voluntary and not all spared the life of the donor. The Mayans sacrificed human beings for many different reasons. Some sacrifices were aimed at appeasing the gods during times of famine, sickness, or war. Other sacrifices were made in hopes of bringing a good harvest.

Carvings and artifacts found at Mayan ruins reveal that some ceremonies demanded a living human heart. A heart might come from slaves or prisoners of war. Sometimes the gods received a heart from select members of Mayan society, including small children, women, or even honored male warriors.

In one ritual, a *chac*—an older, high-ranking priest—held down the victim. A *nacon*, or young priest, would make an incision below the victim's rib cage and rip out the person's heart. The heart was then placed in a sacred bowl and burned. This type of sacrifice took place atop raised platforms or pyramids such as the pyramid of Kukulkan.

## Honorable Death

In another ritual, Mayan warriors (and sometimes prisoners) met in an ancient stone arena nearly the size of a football field. There they engaged in a game in which players tried to toss a ball a little larger than a basketball into great stone hoops. The hoops rose some 20 feet (6 meters) in the air. Players were not allowed to use their hands.

If the winners were enemy warriors, they gained their freedom. The losing side, whether they were Mayans or enemies, lost more than the game. The losers were sacrificed to the gods. Carvings in Chichén Itzá show captives and Mayan warriors being sacrificed after ball court games. The Mayans viewed this type of sacrifice to the serpent god as an honorable death.

Although the pyramid of Kukulkan was important as a place for sacrifice and worship, it also served other functions. It provided ancient Mayan astronomers with a place to study the stars and gave farmers information about when to plant and harvest crops.

Visitors admire the remains of the ball court and stone hoop at the Kukulkan pyramid.

From the top of the pyramid of Kukulkan (pictured), Mayan astronomers tracked the movements of the starts and the planets.

## Marking the Seasons

The pyramid of Kukulkan is the tallest structure in Chichén Itzá. From the top of the pyramid, ancient Mayan astronomers could track the movements of the stars, the moon, and the planets. These astronomers used the pyramid and El Caracol, the ancient observatory in Chichén Itzá, to help the priests plan religious rituals and ceremonies. According to carvings and ancient Mayan hieroglyphs, religious rituals were more powerful when aligned with the movements of the heavens.

Not only did the astronomers use the pyramid to help them study the stars, but rulers also used it to help manage crops. The pyramid was built to function as a large calendar, and rulers kept track of planting and harvest times by watching for changes in the pyramid.

Each of the four sides of the Kukulkan pyramid originally had 91 levels or steps. The 91 steps on each side, plus the platform at the top as the final step, equals 365 steps—the total number of days in a year. There are also 18 sections or terraces on the pyramid, which represent the number of months in the Mayan calendar. Each day, sunset falls on a different step of the pyramid. When the sun shone on a particular step of a terrace, Mayan rulers would instruct farmers to prepare their fields. When the sun shone on a different step on a different terrace, farmers were instructed to harvest those crops.

The pyramid of Kukulkan was a place of great power for the ancient Mayans. They used it as a place of worship, a place of study, and a place of celebration and sacrifice.

Whether to hold treasure, to testify to the strength of a people, or to honor a religious belief, pyramids of the ancient world are as magnificent as they are mysterious. Having stood the tests of time, these ancient pyramids are reminders of cultures and civilizations of long ago.

# Glossary

**architect:** A person who designs buildings and advises in their construction.

**bas-relief:** Carving on a straight or curved surface in which the figures project from the background.

*chac*: An older, high-ranking Mayan priest.

**Egyptologists:** Scientists who study the cultures, peoples, and religions of ancient Egypt.

**enlightenment:** The state of becoming fully aware; a religious state of being.

**hieroglyphics:** Ancient Egyptian writing where pictures and symbols stood for words or actions.

**mastaba:** A large, rectangular-shaped structure built from bricks of mud and straw and used as a tomb for ancient Egyptian rulers.

**mummification:** The process of preparing a body to become a mummy.

*nacon*: A young Mayan priest.

**nomads:** People who roam from place to place to find better living conditions.

**pharaoh:** Absolute ruler or king of ancient Egypt.

**resin:** A transparent or yellowish brown waterproof substance found in certain plants.

**sarcophagus:** A stone coffin.

*shadouf:* A crane used by the Nubians to lift large stones into place for their pyramids.

**step pyramid:** A tall, pyramid-shaped structure made of increasingly smaller levels or steps.

# For Further Exploration

## Books

Brian Innes, *Unsolved Mysteries: Mysteries of the Ancients*. Austin, TX: Raintree Steck-Vaughn, 1999. Discusses mysterious buildings made by ancient people, including the statues at Easter Island and the Great Pyramid at Giza.

Peter Mellett, *Young Scientist Concepts and Projects: Pyramids*. Milwaukee: Gareth Stevens, 1999. Information about ancient pyramids and detailed scientific activities and experiments for young people using pyramid shapes.

## Web Sites

**Archaeology** (www.archaeology.org). Contains articles of archaeological interest by famous archaeologists. Includes articles on ancient pyramids and ancient societies and cultures.

**The Discovery Channel** (http://tlc.discovery.com). Includes information regarding pyramids and cultures of the ancient world—Nubia, Egypt, China, and Central and South America.

**The History Channel** (www.historychannel.com). Includes information on the Moche people and their belief in human sacrifice. Classroom activities and lesson plans about the Moche culture and religious beliefs are provided for teachers.

# Index

# Picture Credits

Cover: Anders Blomquist/Lonely planet Images

Art Today,Inc., 7, 12, 23, 33

© Archivoiconografico,S.A./CORBS, 11, 19

© Jonathan Blair/CORBIS ,18

© Christie's Images/CORBIS ,20

© Michael Freeman/CORBIS ,29

© Historical Picture Archive/CORBIS ,26

© Danny Lehman/CORBIS ,38

© Leonard de Silva/CORBIS ,24

© Hans Georg Roth/CORBIS ,15

© Roger Wood/CORBIS ,17

Lonely Planet Publications 8,9,27,37

# About the Author

A native of Tarboro, North Carolina, Teresa Hyman is a professional editor and writer living in Overland Park, Kansas. She and her husband Derrick are the parents of two children, Briana and Devin. Teresa enjoys researching her African American and Native American heritage and studying the literature and art of those cultures as well.